CONRAD MARCA-RELLI
RECONSIDERED

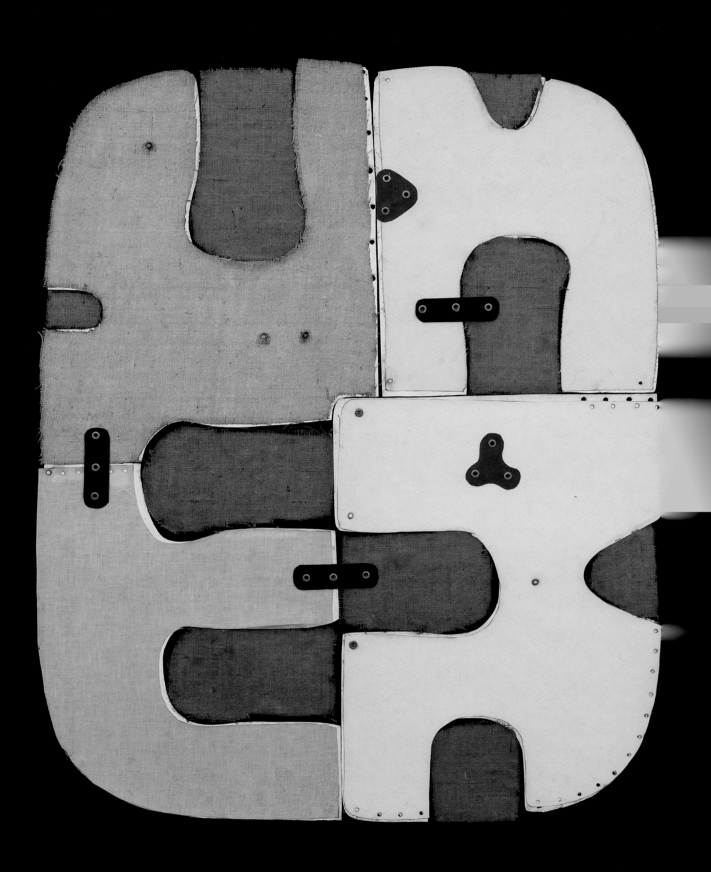

CONRAD MARCA-RELLI
RECONSIDERED

21 January to 5 March 2016

Essay by William C. Agee

HOLLIS TAGGART GALLERIES

521 W 26th Street 7th Floor New York, NY 10001

The Sunday Caller, 1982. Paper and textile collage on paper laid down on canvas, 28 x 34 inches.

The Pool Game (L-I-81), 1981. Oil on burlap, fabric, paper, printed paper, and newsprint collage on canvas, 48 x 55 ⅝ inches.

FOREWORD

Hollis Taggart Galleries has long been committed to exploring the work of artists who deserve reevaluation and further exposure, and as such we have had a long-standing interest in the work of Conrad Marca-Relli. As a core member of the New York School, a founding member of the Eighth Street Club and an organizer of the *Ninth Street Show,* Marca-Relli stood at the center of the New York art world at midcentury. His unique contributions to postwar abstraction embodied the scale and emotional impact of Abstract Expressionism through collage, a medium that had previously been limited in scope. Marca-Relli's innovative use of collage in both large-scale and intimate compositions embodied the spirit of experimentation and individualism that defined this vanguard circle.

As will be discussed in this catalogue, Marca-Relli's work shines in the company of that of his illustrious contemporaries, including Jackson Pollock, Willem de Kooning, and Franz Kline, all of whom he counted as close friends. Beyond his significant contributions to collage, it will be shown that Marca-Relli was a brilliant colorist whose vibrant hues enliven compositions in both oil and collage, as seen in *Untitled* (c. 1949–50) and *Sleeping Figure* (1966), respectively. His singular style deserves an art historical reappraisal, and with that in mind we are proud to present *Conrad Marca-Relli: Reconsidered* as the first postwar exhibition in our new Chelsea location. With this exhibition we reaffirm the gallery's commitment to art historical scholarship and connoisseurship and continue our program of focused, scholarly exhibitions.

We are particularly pleased to have worked on this exhibition with distinguished art historian William C. Agee, who brings a unique voice to the catalogue. He has had the rare opportunity to revisit his thoughts from 1967, when he curated Marca-Relli's first solo exhibition at the Whitney Museum. Agee's 1967 essay has been reprinted in full in these pages, along with a personal and art historical reexamination that illustrates the evolution of both scholar and artist over the five intervening decades. We extend our deepest appreciation and respect to Professor Agee for his compelling insights and his singular perspective.

We would also like to thank Marco Niccoli and his assistant Cecilia Dealessi from the Archivo Marca-Relli for their generosity in sharing information and anecdotes about the artist. Marco's encyclopedic knowledge and dedication to Marca-Relli's legacy are extraordinary. For her continued collegiality, we are grateful to Christine Berry; and we are delighted to include the vintage photo graciously provided by the Estate of Syd Solomon. Many thanks also go to Emily Lembo for her skilled assistance and research. To our colleagues at the gallery who have all made contributions to this project: Dr. Stacey Epstein, Jessie Sentivan, Kara Spellman, Katie Zoni, and particularly to our exhibition coordinator, Ashley Park, we offer our gratitude. For his brilliant design, which we have come to expect, we thank Russell Hassell. We acknowledge Jay Stewart and his staff at Puritan Capital for their expert printing of this catalogue.

Finally, without the personal leadership of Hollis Taggart and his unwavering dedication to scholarship, such exhibitions and catalogues would not be possible. He continues to inspire and challenge us to expand upon the gallery's thirty-year legacy.

Debra Pesci
Martin Friedrichs

Marca-Relli: Then, and Now

By William C. Agee

In 1967, just turned thirty, I was a new associate curator at the Whitney Museum of American Art. I was assigned the responsibility of organizing the retrospective of Conrad Marca-Relli (1913–2000), a longstanding commitment the museum had made some years back. Read my accompanying essay, reprinted here in full. I comment and add to it in the pages that follow. A personal critique, a kind of do–over, which one rarely gets.

Conrad Marca-Relli's achievement has long been to raise collage to a scale and complexity equal to that of monumental painting. Since its inception in 1912 by Picasso and Braque, collage has undergone many formal transformations, yet it has remained a corollary to painting. Even a master collagist, Jean Arp, could refer to collage as a "less-refined" medium. Beginning in 1953, Marca-Relli accepted the potential risks inherent in collage and developed it as a complete pictorial system essentially without precedent in modern art. He has used it neither as a single element of structural reordering of reality as in cubist collage, nor as ambiguous fragments evoking exterior associations as did the Surrealists. Rather, Marca-Relli has extended collage to the point where it now carries its own full and distinct range of formal and emotive means.

In pursuing this course, Marca-Relli has bridged and maintained an uncommon duality of putatively conflicting factors. He has, for instance, virtually abolished the traditional distinction between "representational" and "abstract" by consistently drawing on the figure as a source of abstract images. He has been identified with the second generation of abstract expressionists, yet while employing directness and boldness of the New York School, he has equally espoused traditional values of European painting—polish, elegance and finish—which have been almost universally rejected by other members of his generation. By heritage and temperament Marca-Relli has strong roots in Europe, and at a time when American art has aggressively detached itself from the Continent, he has continued to travel and work there. "I like to travel and I like to visit places that affect me . . . I've been told that it was wrong . . . It's as if you have to do it just here and [must] shut your eyes to other things. I don't believe in shutting my eyes to anything . . . Art is art anywhere."[1]

Marca-Relli is an inveterate and restless traveler. He was born on June 5, 1913 in Boston, and made the first of many extended trips to Europe as a young child with his father, a news commentator and journalist. He began to draw at an early age, was encouraged and given his first lessons in Italy. On these visits abroad Marca-Relli was imbued with a deep feeling for the heritage of Italian culture and the pace and texture of European life, a feeling he has always retained. Eventually the family settled in New York where Marca-Relli finished his last year of high school at night in order to devote more time to painting.

There followed a year of study at Cooper Union after which he enrolled in various small art classes, absorbing the fundamentals of a solid craftsmanship. By this time, in the early 1930's, the Depression had made it increasingly difficult for artists to support themselves. Marca-Relli had by then established his own studio and managed to live by doing occasional drawings and covers for newspapers and magazines, and by a teaching job.

The advent of the WPA art projects in 1935 was, as for so many artists, vitally important to Marca-Relli. From 1935 through 1938 he was employed first as a teacher and then on both the easel and mural divisions of the Federal Art Project. For the first time he was able to support himself while giving his full time and energy to his art. Perhaps more important, however, was that the sense of community developed among artists on the WPA. Marca-Relli came into contact with a new group of acquaintances who were to help in significantly altering his entire view of painting. His supervisor on the mural project was Rollin Crampton; by 1938 among his friends were Peter Agostini, Willem de Kooning, Franz Kline, George Spaventa, John Graham and others. Through discussions and visits to galleries and museums with these artists, Marca-Relli began to absorb the tenets of modernism as revealed in the work of Picasso, Matisse and Miró, as well as Orozco by whom he was briefly influenced in the late 1930's. His break from the prevailing figurative style of the period, however, was halted by his induction into the Army early in 1941. Although he was represented in his first group exhibition, the Soldier–Artists show held that year at the Contemporary Arts Gallery (by a painting entitled *Reveille*), Marca-Relli was unable to work until the war had ended.

After spending a year in Woodstock, he returned to New York in 1946 and resumed painting. Significantly, however, it was in Rome and Paris, where he returned in 1947, that Marca-Relli found the atmosphere in which his first important works were done. These paintings were shown at his first one-man exhibition at the Niveau Gallery in New York in 1947. They were based on circus themes and motifs of Italian Renaissance architecture, and were dominated by expansive dream spaces and elusive surrealist associations of memory. In both the mood and the flat, cutout shapes set into distant perspectives, these paintings were reminiscent of Giorgio de Chirico and Henri Rousseau, artists whom Marca-Relli admired at this time. On the occasion of the exhibition, he remarked, "The lonely street of our childhood, the whistle of the train in the still night, an old circus poster—these are my seeds."[2] These themes were continued until 1949 and were the basis of his second exhibition held that year at the Niveau Gallery. Marca-Relli then began to experiment with another major surrealist vein, a controlled and more formal variation of automatic writing embodied in a series of semi-abstract paintings consisting of protoplasmic and other invented shapes stemming from the unconscious. He extended this direction in 1950–51 with a group of large and totally abstract works shown at the New Gallery in 1951. They were brilliantly colored and animated by a fluid line and biomorphic forms which showed the deep impression Miró and Gorky had made on him. The paintings were successful, but Marca-Relli was displeased with them, feeling that they were not his true direction. In 1951 he traveled again to Rome to question and revaluate the premises of his art.

That year Marca-Relli became absorbed in the texture, solidity and inherent formal order of the architecture of ancient and Renaissance Rome. After returning to New York, he exhibited his new work at the Stable Gallery in 1952. The paintings depicted city squares, ports and buildings, themes which presented a formal context for a rectilinear structure of horizontal and vertical elements. A lingering surrealist mood was evident in the empty and hallucinatory spaces bathed in an eerie light as if glimpsed through a nostalgia for places remembered. Perspectives were sometimes reversed and the effects of weight and gravity accordingly rearranged by darkening skies and treating foreground areas and buildings as volumes of light. The closed, two-dimensional reality of the canvas was emphasized by patterned and interlocking forms brushed in low-keyed, mat blacks, whites, grays, umbers and ochres. Marca-Relli's art, indeed, has proceeded through a logical progression of formal problems suggested by prior investigations. Thus in the paintings of 1952 one can readily perceive a striving for the essence of the physical substance of textures which suggests the literalness and placement of collage forms.

Marca-Relli's art has, moreover, always followed a pattern of moving toward a greater reduction and economy of means. As he increasingly emphasized a taut pictorial structure, he found a kinship with the work of another modern Italian master, Giorgio Morandi, who had realized a vision of harmony and order through very simple but perfect still-life forms. In 1953 Marca-Relli began *Still Life* which, in the path of Morandi, consisted of sparse but full forms suggesting an architectural order. The painting was virtually complete when the artist traveled to Mexico that summer. There he was deeply impressed by the tactile qualities of the brilliantly sunlit surfaces of adobe buildings. This experience led him to renew and intensify his search for the plastic equivalents of the textures and volumes of architecture which had been evident in his painting of 1952. While working that summer Marca-Relli ran out of paint, and as a simple expedient, yet with a logic dictated by the course of his work, he began to experiment with collage. He immediately found that it provided the literal and material density he sought. When he returned from Mexico in the fall, he reworked *Still Life,* attaching strips of plain canvas directly to the table and the oblong form resting on it. He also revised *Seated Figure Outdoors* (p. 38) a painting which had been partially finished before his trip to Mexico. The heavy impasto of this painting indicates his search for the felt qualities of surfaces and textures which collage could resolve simply and directly. By substituting a few areas of canvas it was no longer necessary to build up paint surfaces, which in fact threatened to obscure the underlying order to achieve a structural clarity and firmness.

During the preceding years, Marca-Relli had done, in addition to the architectural themes, a group of figurative works, some of which had been exhibited at the Stable Gallery in 1952. These paintings were the source of his almost exclusive concentration on the figure in the years to follow, a source to which he has constantly returned ever since. In the period from late 1953 through 1955, beginning with

Sleeping Figure of 1953–54, he developed and applied collage as a full pictorial method to a series of single figures. Marca-Relli had moved to East Hampton in 1953 and came in close contact with Willem de Kooning and Jackson Pollock. The figures perhaps owe something to de Kooning's *Woman I* of 1950–51 in which de Kooning pasted together and then tore apart and recomposed collage segments of the anatomy. However, in their adumbrated and faceless anonymity Marca-Relli's manikins are closer in spirit to de Chirico. In these collages, the artist sought what he termed the "architecture of the human figure".[3] He has never worked from the model, preferring to rely on a conceptual process to select and admit only those elements most essential to the creation of the total image.

In seeking the architecture of a single figure, Marca-Relli established the working method which, although later refined, elaborated and sometimes varied, remained as the basis of his art. He started with a rather quickly drawn and rough sketch on the bare canvas to indicate his point of departure, although he did not necessarily hold himself to its confines. He then cut out with a razor blade segments of either raw or primed but unpainted canvas, and later natural or painted linens, which were pinned to the supporting canvas after they had been coated with a mixture of black paint and glue. After they were placed on their foundation, the collage sections were often shifted and rearranged as other segments added in proximity altered the formal relationships within the composition. This method of spontaneous attack with the formal elements in constant flux until the final piece had been secured, allied Marca-Relli with the abstract expressionists. His willingness to accept pictorial accident while controlling it, and to reveal the working process was also in keeping with the tenets of action painting. The process of revising the placement of collage segments frequently meant that several layers of canvas—as many as twenty in one case—were added until he found the desired clarity of the figure. By 1955 Marca-Relli began to add paint to a few of the canvas strips after they had been secured, but limited himself to a subdued cubist palette of ochres, off-whites and grays. Thus collage became a painting with oil and canvas. Another element emerged when the adhesive mixture of glue and paint oozed out and created black outlines which functioned as silhouettes, modifying the relationship between adjoining shapes.

In the collages of 1954–55, such as *Seated Figure* and *Oracle* the figure is flattened against the picture plane in a frontal and hieratic pose. From this position it seems either to move forward or to recede into a shallow and limited background. The use of either alternative to lock the figure in space, creates what he termed a "duality of negative and positive space,"[4] and constitutes a major formal problem in his work at this time. In turn, the interchange of the figure with an indeterminate space creates other opposing forces. Light and dark areas are reversed at points and voids replace implied solids in a cubist inversion of known, objective reality. Each segment of these collage cuts and determines its own place and is relatively large, open, clear and independent, while retaining its place in the whole. Each is imbued with its own kind of geography through the variation of texture, line and silhouette as well as shading of colors. In the works of 1955 such as *The Tenant* the component segments began to shift and overlap as Marca-

FIG I
The Struggle, 1955. Oil and canvas collage, 39 × 73 inches.

Relli's control of the medium was extended and refined. Their easy movement and sliding within the figure's structure left the appearance of an afterimage not quite in focus, which in turn suggested Marcel Duchamp's studies of sequential motion in the *Nude Descending the Staircase* of 1912.

In a series of works initiated by *The Struggle* of late 1955 [fig. 1], Marca-Relli undertook to further extend the expressive range of collage by increasing its complexity and adding to its means. Here, and in other collages, he introduced two figures and sought to establish their architecture. Their relation to the surrounding space became accordingly more intricate and tenuous. Figures broke away from their frontal, seated positions and were depicted in more contorted, active stances which moved diagonally across or down through the canvas. The single figure was by no means abandoned, however, although it too underwent an extensive formal revision as in *The Warrior*. In each case, collage forms became more fragmented and were loosened from the firm and relatively stable vertical and horizontal under-pinnings of the earlier collages. A greater differentiation between line, texture and shape appeared, and more contrasts between painted and unpainted surfaces were also evident. The forms assumed a new biomorphism, in contrast to the earlier simpler shapes; the paint surface became more active and began to pull away from the confines of linear contours. As opposed to the static quietness of the first collages, these works took on a trembling and convulsed motion. The internal movement and new complexity of spatial positioning of these figures was significantly increased by two formal devices used for the first time in *Seated Figure* of 1956. Marca-Relli here experimented with singeing the edges of the canvas strips with a torch to add a fluidity which broke and softened the rigidity of the straight line. In securing the collage segments, he had accidentally spotted the forms with dots of glue, but these had surprisingly incorporated themselves into the overall composition. He thus began to employ them deliberately to simulate rivet holes or track marks. These dots created another element which moved independently over the surface while at the same time binding together the layers of the actual collage.

With his command of collage at a new point of mastery. Marca-Relli began work in 1956 on two large figure compositions, *Trial* and *The Battle* [fig. 2], In these works, he introduced myriad figures in a state of action and movement throughout the composition. They represent what the artist now called "the architecture of an event,"[5] and introduce a multiplicity and complexity unparalleled in his entire career. They combine an extraordinary variety of shapes, textures and contrasts merged in infinite overlappings and intersections which spread across the surface in a series of seemingly unending configurations. The collages done immediately prior to *Trial* and *The Battle* had begun to obliterate recognizable sections of the anatomy, and in these two works virtually all identifiable human references disappeared. The literalness of collage structure became paramount, removing all allusive elements of painting and asserting instead the material hardness of shape, line, shadow and depth. The proliferating forms, while locked together, assumed more biomorphic qualities and were less confined to a precise outline. The artist resumed his dialogue with Italian art in *The Battle*, which was directly inspired by Paolo Uccello's *Battle of San Romano*. Marca-Relli's *Battle* adapted the formal placement of objects in a stilted perspective which was the basis of Uccello's monumental painting. Each segment, like a sword or banner in the Uccello mural, is given its own identity and role in the total compositional scheme. As in the Uccello painting, movement is constant, playing across the accents generated by multiple points of focus.

The next year Marca-Relli returned to a use of the single figure. As in *The Dweller* the human image now became almost completely submerged behind a veil of shredded canvas strips animated by rapid oscillation. In merging with the increasing fragmentation and shattering of these forms, the paint surface was set in motion and worked independently of line and contour to create rippling effects throughout the collage. Marca-Relli took more advantage of accidents incurred in the rapid gluing and painting process, with the result that no one segment existed as a clearly read plane but was merged as part of inseparable junctions.

The density and concentrated energy of these collages were retained in the work of 1958, but were focused to a greater degree within a more constricted area. Figurative references were the basis of *Odalisque* and *Surge*, for example, although they were now completely abstracted. The morphology of the human anatomy was hidden behind a deliberate ambiguity and could be perceived with equal justice as parts of landscape passages. The forces of events and figures in motion became Marca-Relli's concern in these collages, and although the forms were larger, more open and distinct, their convolutions were intensified. The focus on compacted sections seemed to force these shapes into a vortex at

The Battle, 1956. Oil cloth, tinted canvas, enamel paint, and oil on canvas, 70½ × 130½ inches. Image copyright © The Metropolitan Museum of Art. Image source Art Resource, New York.

the center of the canvas. Working on a structural frame which owed something to de Kooning's painting of the late 1940's, Marca-Relli introduced volumes of color as a new formal problem. He abandoned his former subdued range of off-whites and ochres and began applying brilliant reds, blues, and yellows. These hues were sometimes applied as colored linens, but were most frequently painted directly on the canvas surface. A new richness and variation of texture and contrast marked the collages of that year.

After spending a few months during the summer of 1958 in the south of France, Marca-Relli continued to probe the movement of synthesized forces. But his work now embodied the sharp contrasts and greater translucence of Mediterranean light with the result of loosening and opening the compacted density of collage forms. In works such as *Junction* color became thinner and more diffused. Areas of paint were applied independently of contours with the result of simultaneously creating a painting and collage which were merged as separate and distinct entities. As forms broke loose from the earlier density, Marca-Relli opposed the solid reality of collage segments against the illusionism of brushed areas of paint. The spatial atmosphere became more shifting and indeterminate. Shapes within this space were now more linear, clearer and more legible as individual planes. The openness of these works was emphasized by Marca-Relli's reduction of the number of colors to concentrate on the contrast between one dominant hue with strong blacks and whites.

The decreased surface agitation in the work of 1958 pointed to the order and formalism which dominated the collages of the next year. After three years of rapid, even violent movement of forms, Marca-Relli's instinctive urge to a classic stability and harmony reasserted itself in the pattern which has marked the course of his art. In a series of works titled simply by the day on which they were finished, Marca-Relli introduced rectangular shapes which tended to repeat themselves in regular clusters and patterns. These forms were soft and were pervaded by an easy calm as they floated across a single monochromatic field. The infinite breaks and intersections of the earlier collages, as well as the built up layers of canvas and scruffy surfaces and textures, were discarded. In their stead, a simple post-and-lintel arrangement predominated. These collages, although their internal activity was considerably slowed down, were not static; forms within forms were created by spraying black areas within the rectangular shapes which gently shift position and keep the composition from settling into a single given order.

The clarity of structure within these works began to dissolve in 1961, partially through Marca-Relli's renewed investigation of the complexities of the human figure. The duality between figurative and abstract elements at the heart of his work again appeared at this time. In *The Sentinel* for instance, forms based on the figure reintroduced a new biomorphism of interconnecting, irregular shapes which fill the surface with an overall, uniform intensity, marking a new departure for the artist. The regeneration of pictorial complexity found in these configurations of the anatomy were translated into a series of purely abstract collages beginning with *The Passage*, [fig. 3] which can be counted amongst his finest works. In collages such as *Blackboard* and *Monk Brown*, Marca-Relli employed an ambiguity between landscape, figurative and architectural references. Allusions to varieties of perceived experience abound and multiply, moving centrifugally across the surface in expanding and interlooping sections. These shapes were cut quickly and intuitively and combine a sure balance between control and spontaneity. In 1962 Marca-Relli remarked that his method was based ". . . not on speed for its own sake but to create through free, automatic action, before conscious thought can censor out creativeness."[6] These works show a new austerity of color and were limited to gradations of one predominant, resonant hue. The color was sprayed, a method which produced subtle variations of surface density and softened the underlying brittleness and hardness of these forms with a floating, atmospheric luminosity. The effect of contrasts between surface painting and interior collage elements was further modified by the tracing of simulated rivet holes and white lines which divide and re-form additional areas and planes.

The evident hardness in the collages of 1961 forecast a renewed urge to discover again the very substance and tangibility of materials, the impulse which had originally led him to collage many years earlier. Canvas had become almost too pliable, and Marca-Relli now searched for materials which would offer a greater resiliency to the hand. In 1961 he used thin sheets of metal in several small collages, but metal at that time proved too awkward and inflexible. The next year he discovered in sheets of vinyl plastic the right combination of resistance and flexibility. Works of 1962, such as *Plan B* [fig. 4], use

FIG 3
The Passage (L-L-12-61), 1961. Oil, canvas, and mixed media collage on canvas, 84⅛ × 119¾ inches. Photograph by Joshua Nefsky, courtesy of Michael Rosenfeld Gallery, LLC, New York.

vinyl sheets nailed directly to a wooden support. Following his innate tendency to formal reduction and simplicity, the shapes gradually cast off traces of biomorphism and became progressively fewer in number, larger and more open. *Cristobal* and other later works in this series assumed a planar arrangement of horizontal and vertical shapes somewhat reminiscent of the 1959 collages. Volumes of color were added as contrasts to the more neutral and open areas of the natural shades of vinyl. These color volumes also provided a weight which nudges against and displaces other shapes, creating a slow internal rhythm. That rhythm is irregular and offbeat, caused in part by a deliberate awkwardness in cutting and attaching the plastic.

Marca-Relli extended his use of industrial materials in a group of aluminum collages executed in 1963. The even harder, but more graceful medium of aluminum continued to express the literal, tangible qualities of collage, although it carried these works at the same time to a position somewhere between painting and sculpture. The tendency to an economy of means was intensified; these collages rely on a few essential forms cut with clean and precise edges. References to wings, fuselages and tail sections of airplanes are revealed in titles such as *Runway #3* and *Lockheed 200* as well as in the riveted and polished machine surfaces. Marca-Relli has said, "In painting . . . I feel that when I bring it down to

very simple shapes . . . the ambiguous is created."[7] As the aluminum forms move in long, sweeping lines from the edge of the support, or enclose themselves in self-contained shapes, broken only by oblong slivers of color, we are given a subtle pictorial vitality which indeed belies the apparent—and deceptive—simplicity of form.

After the completion of the aluminum collages, Marca-Relli's art followed much the same course as cubist collage of 1912–14. Once the flatness and material reality of the surface had been fully established by a metal skin which prevented spatial recession, the collage could only project itself forward. In 1964, Marca-Relli extended collage into actual, three-dimensional space by means of shallow reliefs which logically had been the direction of collage from its first use in 1912 to Picasso's relief constructions of 1913–14. Marca-Relli's reliefs brought his work to an absolute clarity of minimal parts disturbed only by interior glimpses of mechanical springs which seem to first hold and bind the relief, then imply possibilities of moving, closing or rotating. From this point, Marca-Relli took collage to its ultimate step with a series of free-standing sculptures done in 1966, removing all vestiges of illusionism and transforming collage into a real and physical object. Like the reliefs, the aluminum sections of the sculptures were shaped directly by hand, leaving the unmistakable imprint of the human touch, altering and transforming the materials of the machine.

In 1966, after exploring the possibilities of plastics and aluminum, Marca-Relli returned to paint and canvas as the materials of his collages. Forms in these works were further condensed and colors underwent a parallel modification. Basic contours of the aluminum reliefs were suggested in some cases, as for example, in the rectangular frame within *Untitled*. In this and other collages, whether the shapes were square or oval, forms were open at the center, and were placed directly against large expanses of bare canvas. Some appeared to detach themselves and move freely while others pushed and bulged outward against the frame. Surfaces were subdued and restricted to two or three layers of canvas, painted either a rust, blue-black or deep brown. The opposition of painted canvas to the white background, blemished only by a few ragged edges and paint spots, created a new variation of Marca-Relli's long-standing duality of negative and positive forces. "What happens in the meeting of these forces . . . [which are] like life . . . is for me practically all of the painting,"[8] he says.

More recently, Marca-Relli has brought his work to an even greater economy of means. In the collages of 1967 two or three closed, dense forms are pulled together in an isolated cluster at the center of the canvas. They either intersect or merge completely, leaving the points of contact of the separate collage strips all but indistinct. These collages are infused with a refinement, perfection of finish, and total equilibrium in which all evidence of the working process has been dissolved. Yet at the same time, as he has so often, Marca-Relli has turned again to his constant source of visual fascination, the human figure. That this pattern of rediscovery of the figure, after a drive to a simplified abstraction had tentatively opened a new phase, was apparent in *Figure Form I* of 1966, and one or two collages of 1967. But if these seem isolated examples, Marca-Relli has been working on an extended series of small collage drawings during the past three years which concentrate exclusively on the figure. Like the early collages of 1954–55, these figures are generally seated, and face squarely forward. But unlike them, and in dramatic opposition to the abstract reductions in the 1966–67 work, these collages are filled with a new abundance of brushed and active surfaces and textures. As in his collages done in past years, they strive for an elusive and contingent order, reached by that continuing search which is at the heart of the creative act itself.

Notes
1. Interview with the artist, in Gladys S. Kashdin, *Abstract-Expressionsim: An Analysis of the Movement Based primarily upon Interviews with Seven Participating Artists.* (Unpublished Ph.D. Dissertation, Florida State University, 1965), p 20.
2. Preface to the Catalogue, *Corrado di Marca-Relli*, Niveau Gallery, New York, 1947.
3. Dorothy Seckler, Unpublished Interview with Conrad Marca-Relli, June 10, 1965, Archives of American Art, Detroit [now Washington D.C.].
4. In conversation with the author.
5. Bernard Chaet, "Collage Transformed: An Interview with Conrad Marca-Relli." *Arts.* June 1959, p 64.
6. Harriet Janis and Rudi Blesh, *Collage, Personalities, Concepts, Techniques,* (Philadelphia, Chilton Company, 1962), p 197.
7. Gladys S. Kashdin, op. cit. p 123.
8. Ibid., p 100.

I like the essay and I think I essentially got it right. But now, with close to fifty years of experience, I can see that there were things I missed, or developed insufficiently. Some of this was due to my age, with which came with a certain insensitivity, and a still limited knowledge of contemporary art. I was the self-styled Young Turk, sure of myself, determined to bring the Whitney more into the present. My eyes were on Newman and Judd; Marca-Relli seemed *passé,* even old hat, certainly not mainstream. That is the blindness of youth. So now I say just focus on the artist and the art, nevermind movements, labels, received opinions. You will be pleasantly surprised by what you find. As both Ad Reinhardt and Yogi said, you see a lot just by looking.

In retrospect, the first thing I need to say is that Marca-Relli was a much better artist, the work deeper, richer, more complex, than I first thought. All one needs to do now is go to the Metropolitan Museum of Art in New York and see Marca-Relli's imposing work, *The Battle,* of 1956 (fig. 2), now installed at right angles to one of the certified masterpieces of modern art, *Autumn Rhythm,* 1950, by Jackson Pollock.[1] The proof in the pudding is always in our direct experience of art. This matchup tells us worlds about Marca-Relli, namely that his art holds up with the best. Good art always gets better, and it always wins out. Be sure also to look closely in the present exhibition to smaller, less ambitious works by the artist. We cannot help but be impressed by the delicacy, the subtlety of the handling of color and surface, far more than I was by these same works many years ago. They tell us of the high levels of his painterly skill in executing two very different types of work. First-rate art is marked by just this ability. With age, one's view widens, softening the callowness of youth. We come to understand art not as a river, but as a delta made up of a thousand streams and tributaries, each well worth exploring, and embracing for its own virtues.

I discussed the painterly qualities mixed with the collage, but I now see them as often coeval with the collage itself. This comes as no surprise when we remember that he started as a pure painter, and a very good one at that, as evidenced by his *Untitled,* c. 1949–50 (p. 36). It is a dazzling picture, filled with intense, high-keyed color. The reds may suggest that he had recently seen Matisse's *Red Studio,* 1911, which had been acquired by the Museum of Modern Art in 1949. It quickly became an iconic painting, and was intensely studied by Rothko, but also by untold others, then and later, including Andy Warhol. The sections of Marca-Relli's surface suggest a late cubism such as used by de Kooning, which in turn

FIG 5
Circus, c. 1947. Oil on masonite, 30 x 40 inches.

seem to point to the sections of collage for which he became famous within a few short years. This was evident as early as 1947 in *Circus,* a collection of scattered images, including the section of yellow vertical stripes at right (fig. 5). They appear as a patch cut from another source and applied directly. The stripes clearly reference Mondrian, and, more particularly, Robert Motherwell's painting *Little Spanish Prison,* 1943, acquired then by the Museum of Modern Art. In turn, the drawing and at points the almost vaporized atmosphere will point to his interest in Gorky, who had tragically taken his own life in 1948. So when in 1952–53 Marca-Relli started his collages with their muted, dusty, subdued hues, he had given up a formal and expressive use of color of infinite possibilities. In the early essay, I pointed out that he had said he had taken up collage out of simple necessity, prompted by a lack of materials. But this, I would suggest, is only part of the story. He had given up too much to make the move without deeper reasons. This bears further consideration. That he had turned his back on a gift for uniquely intense color is made clear by *Untitled,* c. 1949–50. He missed color, and felt compelled to indulge in it at least occasionally. The intense reds of *Cristobal* (1962) and *Sleeping Figure (J-L-16-66)* (p. 48), also suggest a renewed if brief engagement with Rothko and Matisse. These paintings have been unknown before now, at least to this writer, and will require further examination of his work from the early 1950s. Could it be that he feared being termed "decorative," in the pejorative sense, the curse that all color painters have had to endure, part of the universal suspicion of color, early on defined by the struggle between Florentine *disegno* and Venetian *colore*? Does this give yet another overlay to the implications of his collage, *The Struggle* (1955, fig. 1)?

This gift for pure painting is apparent even in *The Battle:* its surface activity has a life of its own, moving almost independently from the collage with a variety of strokes and textures that are marvels in their own right. Look closely and we see jabs here and there of intense red, surely a sign of the blood drawn in any battle. The artist may have been referring to, even inspired by Paolo Uccello's *Battle of San Romano,* but he surely was also thinking of World War II, especially the horrible mayhem of June 6, 1944 and the bodies stacked on Utah Beach. I now see such memories in some of Pollock's and de Kooning's work, or even, as a colleague has noted, in the moving bodies of Matisse's collage environment, the multi-paneled *Swimming Pool* (1952), usually assumed to be an idyllic pastoral—but then again, maybe not, maybe more like a Steven Spielberg epic.[2] Good art is always relevant, which I had not yet learned in 1967.

As we look at *The Battle,* we may well be painfully reminded of the unending terrorist attacks that today plague the world, most of all in America—Columbine, Newtown, Oregon, Arizona, next week who knows where. In 1967, I hadn't paid more than passing attention to his subjects, but Marca-Relli had lived through the war, and having been in the service, he seemed to understand the ends to which the world was fast approaching. If we then shift our attention to more intimate and personal struggles implied by a battle, and made explicit in a related painting *The Struggle,* we can dwell on our interior, psychic lives, our sexual drives, and our relations to friends and others. The possibilities are endless, as complex and multifaceted as the interplay of collage and paint. Form and subject are one and the same, and can't be separated, as the best art always is.

Yet collage is still central to Marca-Relli's work, and I stand by my first sentence as to his achievement: he raised collage to the level of monumental painting. This was no small feat. It transformed the medium from a small scaled, intimate type of work to something akin—at its largest, as in *The Battle*—to something with the evocative and visual effect of mural-sized painting. This drive to transform the established scale of easel painting was central to art after 1945. It was at the heart of Pollock's work, as he described it in 1947: ". . . I intend to paint large moveable pictures which will function between the easel and the mural," citing his *Mural* of 1943, which was shown at the Museum of Modern Art in the 1947 exhibition *Large-Scale Modern Paintings.* Pollock could go on to say that he believed "the easel picture to be a dying form, and the tendency of modern feeling is towards the wall picture or mural."[3] He was not alone, for we see this same sentiment, by 1950, in the large canvases of Mark Rothko, Clyfford Still, Barnett Newman, and as it turns out, Marca-Relli, who we must now consider as more central to the art of the time than I had once thought. There are more reasons for this, as well.

In my original essay, I had bypassed any discussion of the older and newer uses of collage, other than the 1912–14 work of Picasso and Braque. But Marca-Relli and collage had not appeared as if by magic, a single-handed feat unto itself. Collage had been extended in the 1920s by Dada and Dada-related artists, including Jean Arp, Hannah Hoch, Kurt Schwitters, and John Heartfield in Europe; and in America by Stuart Davis, John Covert, Joseph Stella, and Arthur Dove, whose astonishing collages of 1925 are among the most radical works of the decade, be it here or in Europe. These works could be

FIG 6
Exhibition catalogue for *Marca-Relli*, at the Whitney Museum of American Art, 1967.

seen at the Phillips Collection in Washington, or at the Yale University Art Gallery as part of the Société Anonyme collection, donated there by Katherine Dreier in 1943. That same year, Peggy Guggenheim organized an exhibition of collage and invited Pollock, William Baziotes, Ad Reinhardt, Alexander Calder, David Hare, Marcel Duchamp, and Robert Motherwell, among others, including the Surrealists, to contribute. Motherwell went on to become an accomplished collagist throughout his life. Others of the burgeoning new American artists would also develop collage, but none made it the basis of his art the way Marca-Relli did. In 1948, the Museum of Modern Art organized a show of collage that included work by the pioneers Picasso, Braque and Arp, the German Dadaists, in particular Kurt Schwitters, and the Surrealists, including Joan Miró. This may well have alerted Marca-Relli to the possibilities offered by the medium. It may also be that the large color cutouts of Matisse first shown in this country in 1948, which impressed everyone and which became a prime source for the art of the late 50s and 60s, had some bearing on Marca-Relli's usage. Looking again at the cover of the Whitney catalogue (fig. 6), with its few shapes and ragged edges, one thinks of the large rectangular color sections in Matisse's *The Snail*, 1952 (Tate Gallery, London) that proceed slowly clockwise around the surface. One also recalls the collages of Robert Rauschenberg, dating from the early 50s, but just as likely he was impacted by Marca-Relli, as vice-versa. Also food for thought.

But perhaps most germane was the art of Alberto Burri (1915–95), a fellow Italian who was developing an art based largely on collage, with a more sculptural materiality than that of Marca-Relli's. Burri used sackcloth, cardboard, even metal as early as 1946, but certainly by 1949, and the work was shown in New York by 1952 at the Stable Gallery where Marca-Relli himself was showing. These pieces were three dimensional, like low relief, in fact emulating the old Italian love of marble and stone, its weight and its density forming the very basis of classic and Renaissance sculpture, and even architecture, the mother of the arts. Remember that architecture was always in Marca-Relli's thinking; he referred to some works as the "architecture of the figure" and others as the "architecture of an event," having evolved from his early paintings built around houses. It is therefore not surprising that Marca-Relli's placement of his collage segments will remind us of a mason or stone cutter building up his architectural surfaces. These are the materials and art forms that can be found to this day as one walks through any historic city or village in Italy. The tradition was seared into any Italian artist, Burri and Marca-Relli among them. For both, collage provided a rock solid foundation on which to forge their own experience, for form is content, and vice versa. Burri's works with cloth were made of jute sacks, which he brought with him from the POW camp in Texas in which he was held during the war. As Emily Braun has memorably written, the textures of these works suggest the texture of the human body.[4] As Marca-Relli did later, Burri also used fire to transform materials, in what Mariolina Bassetti termed "a violent act comparable to birth."[5]

However, make no mistake, Marca-Relli combined collage and painting in unique ways; his method was sui generis as William Rubin described it in 1959.[6] While many of his most notable works were on the grand scale, he was remarkably adept at exploring a smaller, more intimate world. In a canvas not even two feet square, done in September 1959 while in the south of France, we seem to be reliving his most private life. The ochre colors suggest the Provençal landscape and houses, with scattered patches recalling the sky and water, the languid atmosphere of the Mediterranean. We know this since the painting is inscribed on the stretcher "X-9-1-59" followed by "Villa Horizon" (p. 44), referring to a resort still in existence. Yet stabbing into and between these areas are sharp wedges of red, suggesting something else, something of the human heart, of human passions. This may remain a puzzle; but when we are reminded that a work of art is an organic whole, we turn the canvas over, and examine the back (fig. 7). There it is: another collage, made up solely of carefully cut and arranged segments from a French newspaper, pasted to the reverse. Look again at the front—the paste and the newsprint have darkened parts of the surface, with some of the newsprint now showing through, if only barely discernibly. The collage on the verso is not complete by any means, but its connection to the front is incontrovertible. There it is—shades of de Kooning's *Easter Monday* (1955–56, The Metropolitan Museum of Art) or Jasper Johns' *Flag* (1954–55, The Museum of Modern Art), both with their famous newsprint embedded in the surface, plain to see. The work has slightly darkened, a literal embodiment of time and its effects, a topic now currently discussed widely. But Marca-Relli's reverse collage is much different, for he has meticulously glued a specific message through words cut from advertisements. This is no accident, for it is too carefully crafted. (Remember Pollock's admonition; "no accidents"[7] and "no chaos, damn it."[8]) We also

FIG 7
Verso of *Villa Horizon* (*X-S-1-59),* see page 44.

remember the explicit messages Picasso and Braque embedded in their collages.[9] Further, to clinch the case, he has added deliberate swaths of turquoise to fill out and support the newsprint, to make sure we understand this as a distinct work of art, even if it is not complete. Often, a work of art is finished when it is finished enough. The message stares us in the face, for reading from left to right and top to bottom, or bottom to top and right to left, it is all the same. "La vie . . . Avis N'Oubliez Pas . . . l'amour." [Life . . . Attention don't forget . . . love.] At the end of the August *vacance*, he records a personal, maybe bittersweet, or joyous, (or both, as life is), message to us, only now discovered. We then turn the picture over again, to study further the imagery there. It is hard to read, but it does begin to encircle itself, encouraging focus on the exact center, as the Renaissance artist did, and often the modern artist as well. Cézanne's grand bathers do this, and, more literally of course, so do Noland's first circles of exactly the same time. Within this rough circle of Marca-Relli's composition can we discern, even if roughly, the embrace of two figures that refer to the back, and vice versa? And to think we still hear people who insist that abstract art is divorced from real life.

The relation between Burri and Marca-Relli also tells us again just how important the interaction between Europe and the United States was in the development of modern art in New York and America. We have been so bent on proclaiming the triumph of American art after 1945—as if it appeared by magic, a product of a Big Bang—that we have forgotten just how varied and international were its sources. Indeed, the very idea of the New York School seems odd, since only two of it members, Newman and Gottlieb, were even from New York. The others were provincials who came to New York to better themselves, from Indiana, Washington state, California, and in Marca-Relli's case, from Boston by way of Italy. The idea was to get away from "French polish," as David Smith termed it,[10] or to just break free from Europe and the old order as both D.H. Lawrence[11] and Donald Judd insisted. But no one can ever escape their roots; it's in our artistic and personal DNA, and the older we get the more we want to (re) connect with our early lives, for that is where we learned the things that shaped us. Remember also that a good portion of Abstract Expressionism was generated from 1948 on, not in New York, but in Paris, and in California as well. Sam Francis was formed in his native San Francisco but his art came to full maturity in France, via the lessons he could take from Monet and Renoir, and later from Van Gogh. Ellsworth Kelly, a youthful leader of the Hard-edge school that formed a parallel, alternate history with Abstract Expressionism, was shaped in good part by Paris and his encounters with Monet's blues. He also developed a personal kind of collage.

With this in mind we need give more attention to Marca-Relli and his classical roots in Italy. They were deep and strong, as I outlined in my original essay. Indeed, I have come to understand over the years that the classical has played a much larger part in modern art than we have realized. Classic or classical means many things; but it starts with the ideal of calm, order, and serenity as fundamental to art; the old idea that modern art was based on upheaval, revolution, and destruction of the past actually only applies to any extent to the Futurist agenda of 1912–18. Equally important has been an art of meditation and contemplation, as in the art of Matisse and Rothko and many others. It goes back to Titian and Poussin and extends through our age. It espouses an art of clarity, order, and sureness, as in Cocteau's famous "call to order."

A drive to these ideals began in 1916 in the midst of the disasters of World War I. The slaughter of hundreds of thousands of men, including artists and critics such as Guillaume Apollinaire, urged artists to turn to a new type of art in which to make a new world and society. Artists would reject the multiple fractured forms of pre-war abstraction, seen as willful and undisciplined, and in its place turn to an art of classical calm, well-constructed, like an architect builds a house, exercising their will by making models of clarity and order.[12] The new art was meant to replace the insanity of war and the society that brought it about. The art could be figurative as in Picasso's monumental classical figures done in Rome from 1917–23, or as lean and abstract as Mondrian, whose art could be the model of literally building a new world. In my original essay[13] I compared Marca-Relli's single figures to manikins, a kind of figure of speech. It turns out I was right, more so than I could have imagined. In a photo of 1954 we see an artist's manikin hanging on the wall of his studio (fig. 8). Each body part is loose and can be moved separately, allowing the artist to set up any pose he desires. No wonder he could speak of the "architecture of the figure." It is a practice as old as the hills, a modern offshoot of the écorché, the model used by artists to study human anatomy.

FIG 8 Marca-Relli in his home-studio, East Hampton, 1954. Photograph published in Anfam, et. al. *Conrad Marca-Relli* (Milan: Bruno Alfieri, 2008), 51.

We know that de Kooning had occasionally used a manikin in his male figure paintings of the late thirties, but it now appears that Marca-Relli had regularly incorporated it in his practice as well.

Marca-Relli, as many others did in the twenties, used Old Master models, a single figure alone, as in *Sleeping Figure (J-L-16-66)*, 1966, which cannot only conjure up, but indeed directly references such famous works as Michelangelo's sculpture *Night* (1526–31) that graces the tomb of Giuliano de Medici in the New Sacristy, San Lorenzo, Florence; Giorgione's *Sleeping Venus* (c. 1510) in the Gemäldegalerie Alte Meister in Dresden; and Titian's *Venus of Urbino* (1538) in the Uffizi Gallery, Florence. The reclining nude, usually seen as a representation of the delicate balance between sacred and profane love, could also symbolize a return to order experienced by artists during the Renaissance, the desire to recreate a lost Golden Age,[14] Renaissance artists often looked back to Rome and Greece. Praxiteles was the first to sculpt Aphrodite completely nude after the Greeks were hesitant to do so. She has one hand covering her body and her head is turned to the side, she exudes eroticism and surprise after we have just caught her in the bath. She is perfectly proportioned and displays emotion, and that emotion is Pandora; for once emotion is set free order collapses on its own weight both in classical Greece and in the Italian Renaissance. This is also the tangential point when the sacred and profane merge to the ultimate detriment of the sacred, the stoic gods being no match for the sensitive beings who invented them. With the Renaissance came a resurgence of the female nude beginning with Giorgione's *Sleeping Venus*. This lineage carries on with Velazquez's *Rokeby Venus* (c. 1647–51) in the National Gallery, London; Goya's *La Maja Desnuda* (c. 1797–1800) in the Prado Museum, Madrid; Manet's *Olympia* (1863) in the Musee d'Orsay, Paris; and continues into the 20th century with Matisse's multitude of nudes, for instance his *Pink Nude* of (1935) in the Baltimore Museum of Art; all the way up to and past Marca-Relli's 1957 collage, *Odalisque*, in the Albright-Knox Art Gallery.

As an artist who fervently looked back to the Old Masters, Marca-Relli's collages *Sleeping Figure* and *Odalisque* also recall Michelangelo's unfinished *Slaves* (c. 1520–23; c. 1530–34) in the Accademia Gallery in Florence. Just as the contorted Slaves desperately try to break free from their marble confines, Marca-Relli's figures, trapped by the forms surrounding them, attempt the same path to freedom, but this time from the canvas. We are also reminded of how Matisse acted as a sculptor with his scissors when he liberated various forms from colored paper in order to construct his cut-outs.

So, too, could Marca-Relli's *Seated Figure Outdoors* (1953, p. 38) have taken its cues from Michelangelo's sculpture of *Moses*, located in the Church of San Pietro in Rome, just thirty minutes walking distance from both of the studios he rented on Via Margutta and Via del Babuino in the late forties and early fifties. Marca-Relli's single robust collaged figure, exuding the grandeur intrinsic to Michelangelo's sculpture, conveys an unspoken formidability with its strong, seated posture. The figure's exaggerated musculature, indicated at the upper arms by rotund swaths of collage, indeed is reminiscent of Michelangelo's herculean marble figures. Marca-Relli most likely was exposed to other monumental seated figures during his time in Italy, such as Nanni di Banco's *Saint Luke* (c. 1408) and Donatello's *Saint John the Evangelist* (c. 1409–11), both in the Florence Cathedral.

Other references from past history abound: medieval history as in *The Joust* (1959) and *The Oracle* (1955), in addition to other classical and Renaissance references as in *Ajax* (1956) and *The Warrior* (1956),

FIG 9 Conrad Marca-Relli and Syd Solomon, East Hampton, 1965. Photo: Courtesy Estate of Syd Solomon.

and even *St. Cyprian's Day* (1957–58). Other cultures appear. In my 1967 essay, for example, I spoke of how influential Mexican architecture and its adobe coloration was on his mature work. Though not exactly classical, it serves as another example of how Marca-Relli was a world traveler and how different cultures could seep into his work. This is distinctly American of course, which Marca-Relli ultimately is— absorbing and assimilating the textures of cultures from around the world, even from places as far away as Japan, as is evident in *The Samurai* of 1957.

The artist's affinity for sculpture and the antique dates to his earliest involvement with making art. In 1927, Marca-Relli was accepted as an apprentice to the Italian sculptor Onorio Ruotolo (1888–1966) where he was responsible for keeping unfinished clay sculptures wet at Ruotolo's studio on East 14th Street. After a while, he was finally allowed to paint in a corner during his free time, and there began his training as a young artist. He would also often listen to Ruotolo speak openly about his feelings about art and life during lunch breaks.

By 1930, Marca-Relli had enrolled in classes at Cooper Union, and from there joined a class of art students, led by the artist Faust Azzaretti (1900–85), that met in a studio in the same building as Ruotolo's three nights a week. Azzaretti ran a strict class and he emphasized the diligent copying of Old Master prints. Each student was to work on copying a print for at least one month. The art of copying, a practice that originated during the Renaissance, was a crucial learning tool for young artists refining their technical skills (for instance, Michelangelo spent a great deal of his early training copying Verrocchio's work in a notebook). At Azzaretti's studio, students were instructed to copy a print of their choosing with silverpoint pencil and bone paper. Marca-Relli, who chose a Michelangelo torso from a group of various Old Master prints after he was attracted to "its flexing muscles," was then instructed by Azzaretti to select the prints that did not interest him. Among these rejections was a head by Bellini, which Marca-Relli found "boring." When Azzaretti heard this, he insisted that Marca-Relli copy it instead of the Michelangelo torso. "I was very angry at the prospect of spending a month copying a work that did not interest me. At the end of a month, I had learned to love Bellini and learned something about art that I was to remember for the rest of my life."[15]

Little wonder, then, that, as he later recalled, he resisted abstraction because he was so dedicated to the classical figure. We call this academic, but that is the wrong term. It is conservative in the best sense, wanting to preserve what is best in older art but using it as a foundation for one's own personal explorations. Marca-Relli was not alone in this course. The students in Matisse's class in 1907 were shocked by the master's insistence on drawing from antique casts; and in 1908 when Matisse was worried that his art had become too impressionistic, he went back to Italy to restudy the Old Masters. By that fall his art emulated in his own way the bulk and solidity of Giotto, Piero della Francesca, and Michelangelo.

Pollock developed his own expressionism in the late thirties by using Old Master reproductions as the basis for extracting his own powerful impulses. De Kooning, from the country that invented oil painting, only seldom veered away from the figure, and was well aware of the discipline of older art, as indicated by his famous essay, "The Renaissance and Order." He put it well when he spoke of the "train track back into the history of art that goes back to Mesopotamia . . . Duchamp is on it, Cézanne is on it.

Picasso and the Cubists are on it, Giacometti, Mondrian, and so many, many more—whole civilizations."[16] Marca-Relli clearly saw things in the same way.

Many of these works embody or refer to a single figure, engaged in or about to engage in a struggle of what kind we cannot always be sure. But they do point to a theme both classical and modern, or even universal: that of man alone in the world facing the forces of nature and even the gods. Think of the Greek heroes setting out on their own. In America this has special meaning, for its theme has been fundamental to the new world since its discovery and runs throughout our art and literature: man confronted with the vastness of the space of the continent. How does he come to terms with it? It is an elusive question, but many artists and writers have seen it as an existential battle: man alone, confronting nature. Think of David Smith's field of sculptures in Bolton Landing, standing individuals in rugged nature and wilderness, alone with their own thoughts. John Donne could say "no man is an island," but in America there is no such thing. In *Moby Dick,* Melville famously proclaims that indeed, every man **is** an island, an *isolatoe,* as he called him, living in his own world, with his own thoughts, unconnected to others. Lincoln's father, the myth goes, moved every time he saw the smoke from a neighbor's cabin. A rugged individual to be sure, but it instantly destroys any sense of community. One may wonder if Marca-Relli identified with some of these figures, seeing in them a parallel with his own journey from the old world to America. Or perhaps he saw this as a way of straddling both worlds, for he often returned to Italy for extended periods.

Classicizing art would restore a sense of harmony and calm often through careful post-and-lintel construction, which we see in more than a few of Marca-Relli's collages of the late fifties such as *October 27, 1959* and *16 November, 1959.* This gave a much different mood to his work, a more relaxed tenor, also apparent in the work of other artists after the death of Pollock in 1956. Marca-Relli had been especially close to him and had the grisly task of identifying his body after the fatal crash. He was also in debt to Pollock and his work, as was virtually every other artist of the time. After Pollock's death, expressionist art began to open up, to move away from the heavy surfaces of the early fifties, which had begun to produce work that came to be seen as too dense, too overworked. As they always had at such moments, artists sought a new clarity, a new harmony, a new simplicity. It is a good example of Ockham's razor, of the artist, like the scientist, seeking the most elegant solution to a problem.

In his famous essay of 1958, "The Legacy of Jackson Pollock,"[17] Allan Kaprow saw art as moving into real space, the same conclusion drawn by Donald Judd, although with completely different results. By 1960, younger artists such as Frank Stella, Kenneth Noland, and Judd himself had moved to new formats of a more reductive nature. Marca-Relli and others of his generation did the same. (Think of de Kooning's *Door to the River,* 1960, with its open, broad structure.) Soon Marca-Relli was working in three dimensions with industrial materials that represented a distinct innovation for him. Aluminum, as used in aircraft, became his favorite material. With this thin, light and tensile medium he could get a kind of minimalist structure, but one that, unlike Judd's boxes, had distinct references to the culture, such as air and travel. Little wonder, since he was a frequent international traveler, that titles such as *Lockheed 200* (1964) and *Runway #3* (1963) command our attention, all incorporating ideas of speed and a new age of rapid international travel. Judd, in a review of a 1964 show of Marca-Relli's, astutely noted that the freestanding metal pieces were held together by pegs, some with springs around them, so that the "reliefs look like mechanisms, look as if the plates should slide together and apart and the holes open and close."[18] This puts these pieces in an entirely new light, referring perhaps to machine paintings for example by Morton Livingston Schamberg and Charles Sheeler. Their formats point to other famous works, both sculpture and painting. In Marca-Relli's *X-L-20-70* from 1970 (p. 56), four puzzle-like shapes, two made of light brown burlap on the left and two made of white canvas on the right, are arranged to create four main quadrants that become one vertical rectangular form with rounded edges. A dark brown colored burlap fills in the negative space within the collage, allowing the forms to appear as if they are interlocking, recalling Brancusi's sculpture *The Kiss* (1916), in particular when the profiles of Brancusi's male and female figures are viewed head on, from left to right. From this angle, four rectangular quadrants are created, divided by the two arms that embrace each other. These figures are so perfectly entwined with one another that they form one whole sculpture, making it difficult to discern just where one figure ends and the other begins.

In Marca-Relli's 1966 *Untitled,* an ovular shaped black collage form embraces a smaller, warped circular form on a white horizontal canvas. Arthur Dove's "Sunrise" series of 1936–37 comes to mind, particularly *Sunrise III* (Yale University Art Gallery), where circular rings of various colors, some of them dark, others light, imitate the glow of the sun against the sky. We also think of Kenneth Noland's circle paintings of the mid- to late-fifties, and his embryo-like shapes originating at the exact center of the canvas, multiplying themselves and expanding towards the outer edges of the frame. By the mid-sixties, Marca-Relli clearly shared the concerns of a younger generation in their drive toward a more formal, focused, and clarified type of art.

Judd also noted that it was important for Marca-Relli to try something new, which is certainly true, but I felt they were at odds with what I thought of as their essential sensibility: the handmade, the touch and workings of the hand in motion, the painterly. That he had abandoned this mode by 1966 indicates that he felt the same way, returning—for the best, I think—to his more familiar mode of collage, canvas, and paint. I wish I had asked him more about this. Conrad, thanks for reminding me that good art wins. Always. Hollis, too, for a chance to give this fine artist his full and proper due. He deserves it.

Esteemed scholar and curator *William C. Agee* is the Evelyn Kranes Kossak Professor of Art History, Emeritus, at Hunter College and has published widely on American art. He has held curatorships at the Museum of Modern Art and the Whitney Museum of American Art, and museum directorships at the Museum of Fine Arts in Houston and the Pasadena Art Museum. His forthcoming book, *Modern Art in America 1908–1968,* will explore the many artists, movements, histories, and other forces that shaped a critical period in American art.

Notes

This essay was produced with additional research by Emily Lembo.

1. See David Anfam, "A Sum of Destructions," in *Conrad Marca-Relli* (Milan: Bruno Alfieri, 2008), 30.

2. Conversation with Sasha Janerus, Fall 2014.

3. Jackson Pollock, application for the 1947 Guggenheim Fellowship. Reprinted in Pepe Karmel, *Jackson Pollock: Interviews, Articles, and Reviews* (New York: Abrams, 1999), 17.

4. See Emily Braun and Carol Stringari, "Sacchi," in Emily Braun, Megan M. Fontanella, and Carol Stringari, *Alberto Burri: The Trauma of Painting*, exh. cat. (New York: Guggenheim, 2015), 156–81.

5. Mariolina Bassetti, as quoted in "Alberto Burri: 'Artist, Poet, and Creator of the New," *Christie's Daily* (October 7, 2015), http://www.christies.com/features/Alberto-Burri-Artist-poet-and-creator-of-the-new-6584-1.aspx?PID=newsviews_landing_morefeatures3.

6. William Rubin, essay for "Marca-Relli, New Paintings: February 9–February 20, 1959" (New York: The Gallery, 1959).

7. Jackson Pollock, narration for Hans Namuth and Paul Falkenberg's film, *Jackson Pollock* (1951).

8. Pepe Karmel (ed.), *Jackson Pollock: Interviews, Articles and Reviews* (New York: Museum of Modern Art, 1999), 71. On December 11, 1950, Pollock wrote this in a telegram to the editor of *Time* after the magazine had quoted an Italian critic's description of his paintings as "chaotic."

9. See my essay, "Looking at Braque," *New Criterion* (February 1983), 51–56.

10. 'Questions to Students' typescript c. 1953–4, David Smith Papers, Archives of American Art, Smithsonian Institution, Washington, DC.

11. D.H. Lawrence, "Chapter I: The Spirit of Place," in *Studies in Classic American Literature* (New York: T. Seltzer, 1923).

12. See my forthcoming book, *Modern Art in America: 1908–1968*, out March 21, 2016 from Phaidon.

13. See my 1967 essay on Marca-Relli, reprinted on pp. 9–19. Essay originally published for the Whitney Museum of American Art. See Agee, "Marca-Relli," (New York: Whitney Museum of American Art, 1968), 13.

14. Conversation with Emily Lembo, Fall 2015.

15. Conrad Marca-Relli, "I remember when . . . ," unpublished autobiography, written between 1950s–1980s. Reprinted in David Anfam et al., *Conrad Marca-Relli* (Milan: Bruno Alfieri, 2008), 48.

16. Willem de Kooning, "The Renaissance and Order," lecture delivered at Studio 35, autumn 1949. Reprinted in Thomas B. Hess, *Willem de Kooning* (New York: The Museum of Modern Art, 1968), 141–43.

17. Allan Kaprow, "The Legacy of Jackson Pollock," *Art News* 57, no. 6 (October 1958).

18. Donald Judd, "In the Galleries: Conrad Marca-Relli", *Arts Magazine* (November 1964). Reprinted in *Donald Judd: Complete Writings 1959–1975: Gallery Reviews, Book Reviews, Articles, Letters to the Editor, Reports, Statements* (Halifax: Press of the Nova Scotia College of Art and Design, 1975), 143.

Untitled, c. 1949–50
Oil on canvas
60 x 80 inches

Seated Figure Outdoors, 1953
Oil and collage on canvas
21¼ x 15 inches
Private collection

Collage #55, 1957
Oil on canvas with canvas collage
36 x 52 inches
Private collection

Villa Horizon (X-S-1-59), 1959
Oil and collage on canvas
21 x 23 inches

F-S-18-66, 1966
Oil and collage on canvas
20½ x 16¼ inches
Private collection

Sleeping Figure (J-L-16-66), 1966
Oil, charcoal, and canvas collage on canvas
53 x 60 inches

F-S-8-67, 1967
Oil and collage on canvas
21¾ x 17¾ inches

Untitled (F-S-25-67), 1967
Collage on canvas
24 x 28 inches

X-L-30-69, 1969
Mixed media on canvas
56½ x 68½ x 1¼ inches

X-L-20-70, 1970
Collage on canvas
69⅛ x 57 x 1½ inches

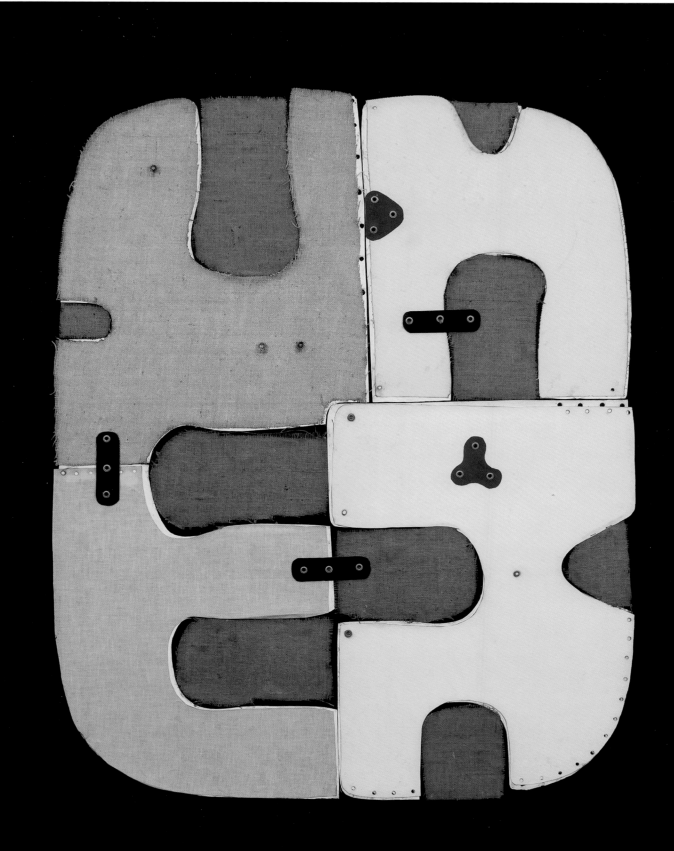

Untitled, 1973
Collage on canvas
13⅝ x 19¾ inches

Untitled, 1973
Collage on canvas
13½ x 14 inches

Untitled #4, c. mid-1970s
Mixed media on canvas
56¾ x 68 inches

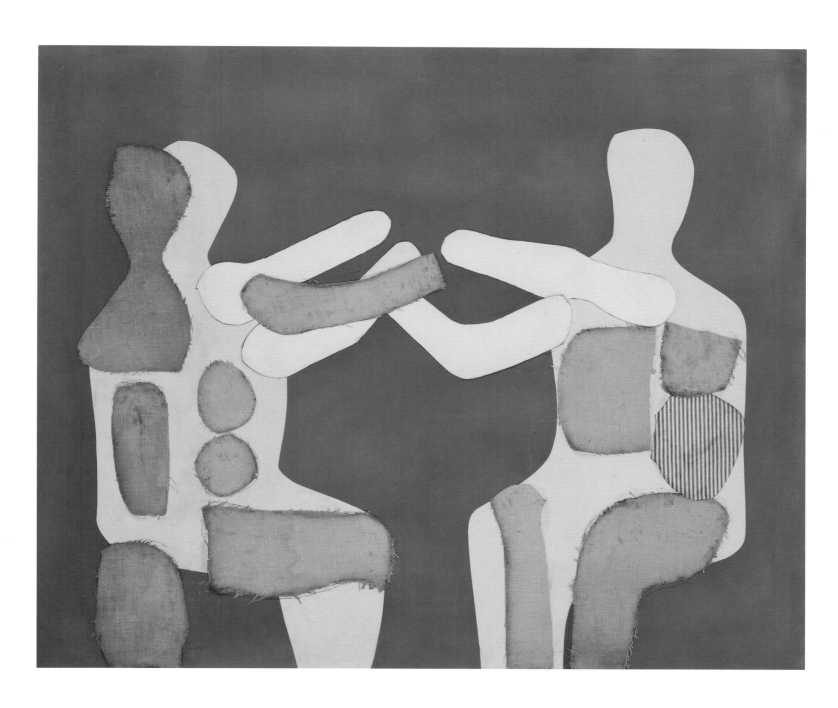

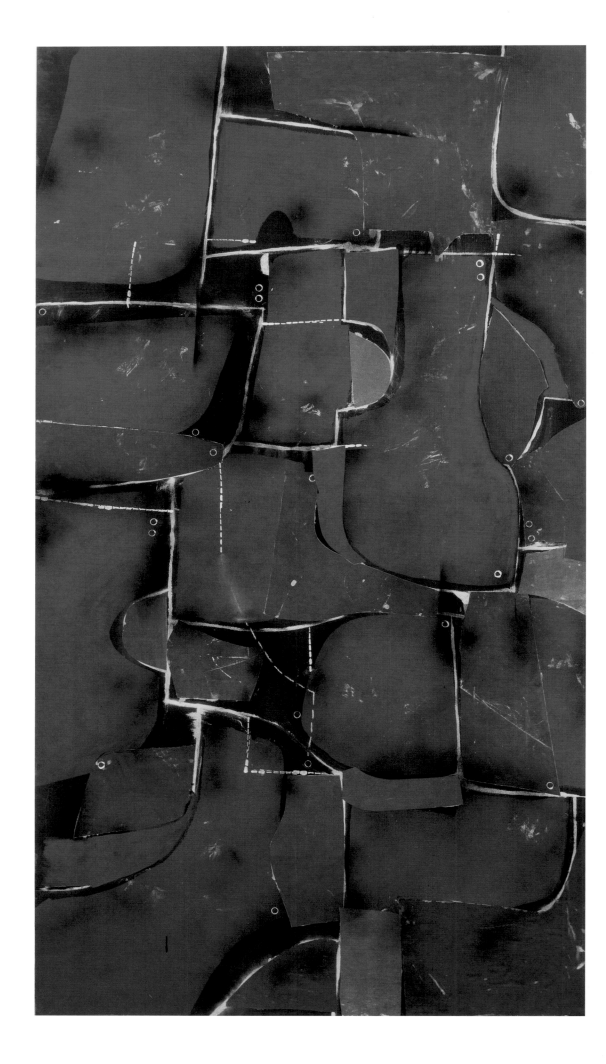

Black-Board 2 (L-L-1-84), 1984
Oil on canvas collage on canvas
91 x 100 inches (diptych)

This catalogue has been published on the occasion of the exhibition
"Conrad Marca-Relli: Reconsidered," organized by Hollis Taggart
Galleries, New York, and presented from January 21 to March 5, 2016.

ISBN: 978-0-9889139-0-5

Front cover: *Sleeping Figure (J-L-16-66)*, detail, 1966, pp. 48–49
Pages 6–7: *Untitled*, detail, 1973, p. 58
Frontispiece: *X-L-20-70*, 1970, p. 56
Back cover: *X-L-30-69*, detail, 1969, p. 54

Hollis Taggart Galleries
521 West 26th Street, 7th Floor, New York, NY 10001
Tel 212 628 4000 Fax 212 570 5786
www.hollistaggart.com

Catalogue production: Ashley Park
Design: Russell Hassell, New York
Printing: Puritan Capital, New Hampshire
Photography: Josh Nefsky, unless otherwise noted

All images courtesy of the Archivo Marca-Relli, Parma, unless
otherwise noted.

HOLLIS TAGGART GALLERIES

Chelsea 521 W 26th Street 7th Floor NY, NY 10001   **Private Viewing** 18 E 64th Street 3F NY, NY 10065   212 628 4000   hollistaggart.com